More Knitted Lace

This book is for our guardian a... ...en who have shared with us some of the r... ...s of our career and have been there for u... past few years while enduring and overcoming their own ou... wisdom and strength has shown us that we are capable of dealing with all the difficult and sometimes unfair situations of life, simply by believing in ourselves and getting on with life.

Vicki Moodie.

Copyright: R & V Moodie   1998

All rights reserved. Except as provided under the copyright act, no part of this book may be reproduced in any form or by any means, including photocopying, without permission in writing from the author.

ISBN 1 876373 01 6

Published by

CRAFT MOODS
P.O. Box 1096
CABOOLTURE Qld. 4510
Australia

Phone/Fax (07) 5496 6826
www.craftmoods.com.au

Printed by   NICHOLSON PRINTERS Pty Ltd
Unit 6C
43 Morayfield Road
CABOOLTURE Qld. 4510

Phone (07) 5495 1371
Fax (07) 5498 3783

6/00

CONTENTS

Page

Abbreviations	2
Types of Eyelet Lace	3
General Instructions	3/4

PATTERNS:

1.	Maroon & Cream Coat-hanger	5
2.	Brown & Cream Coat-hanger	6
3.	Apricot & Cream Coat-hanger	7
4.	Green & Cream Coat-hanger	9
5.	Arrow Head Coat-hanger	10
6.	Dusty Pink & Cream Coat-hanger	12
7.	Hair Clip Tidy	15
8.	Poodle Doorstop	18
9.	Doorstop Dolly	25
10.	Butterfly Magnets	30
11.	Tooth Fairy	32
12.	Doll's Carry Bassinet	34
13.	Evening Clutch Purse	36

ABBREVIATIONS

K	knit	tog	together
m1	make one (see below)	st(s)	stitch(es)
P	purl		

Make one (m1): Knit a stitch into the loop between stitches on left and right needles.

Garter stitch: All rows knitted.

Stocking stitch: One row knit, one row purl.

TYPES OF EYELET LACE (85 holes/m actual size)

GENERAL INSTRUCTIONS

HOW TO KNIT IN LACE
From the left, place lace to back of work, insert needle into the first stitch and through first eyelet hole in lace, yarn over needle and complete the stitch. Keep the tension loose. Follow this procedure to end of row and cut off lace only.

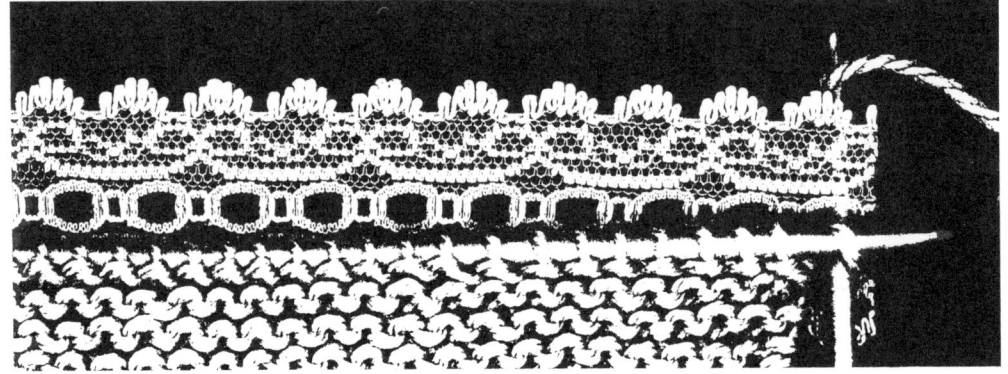

TO NEATEN and JOIN: To neaten ends of lace rows, overlap lace towards you by one hole at the beginning and the end of the row. To join eyelet lace part way through a row, just overlap each piece of lace by two sets of holes.

HOW TO PLEAT LACE

Cut specified number of lace pieces to the required length (or number of holes) as per pattern instructions. When pleating lace, the lace is held at right angles, up from the knitting, and each length of lace is knitted into every second row as per the pattern instruction "pleat lace".

To "pleat lace", place lace to back of work so lace is at right angles, up from the work, insert needle into the pleat stitch and through two eyelet holes in lace, yarn over needle and complete the stitch. Continue with plain knitting until next "pleat lace", and pleat in the next piece of lace. Continue in this manner to end of row.

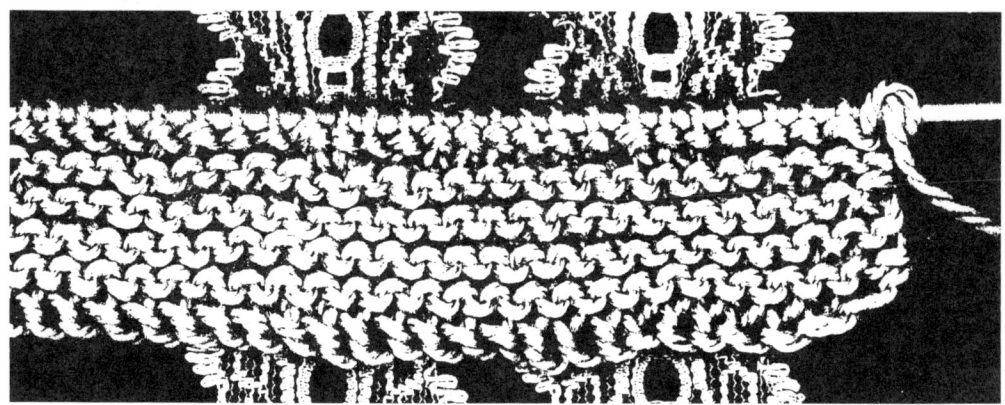

OTHER METHODS TO COVER COAT-HANGER HOOKS

1. Thread 4mm plastic tubing over hook and finish with a plastic tip.

2. Thread hook with 1.5cm wide gathered lace (with a header large enough to insert the wire hook) and glue into place.

3. Knitted in lace:
    Cast on 25sts.
    Knit 3 rows.
    Knit in a row of double sided eyelet lace. Cast off.
    Right sides out, sew cast-on and cast-off edges together. Thread over hook and sew or glue into place.

4. Wrap hook with 6mm wide ribbon and glue ends into place.

1. MAROON & CREAM COAT-HANGER

2.6m (220 holes) double sided eyelet lace [85 holes per metre]
8ply yarn
pr 3.75mm knitting needles
padded adult coat-hanger

Note: Overlap lace by 2 holes at each end to neaten.

Cast on 68sts.

Knit 3 rows.

Row 4. Knit lace into 12sts, K16, knit lace into 12sts, K16, knit lace into 12sts.

Knit 5 rows.

Row 10. K12, knit lace into 16sts, K12, knit lace into 16sts, K12.

Knit 7 rows.

Row 18. K12, knit lace into 16sts, K12, knit lace into 16sts, K12.
(3 rows of lace)

Knit 5 rows.

Row 24. Knit lace into 12sts, K16, knit lace into 12sts, K16, knit lace into 12sts. (4 rows of lace)

Knit 3 rows. Cast off.

Make up instructions on Page 11.

2. BROWN & CREAM COAT-HANGER

2.4m (200 holes) of double sided eyelet lace [85 holes per metre]
8ply yarn
pr 3.75mm knitting needles
padded adult coat-hanger

Note: Overlap lace by 2 holes at each end in rows 2 and 28 to neaten. Cut 5 pieces of lace each 33 holes in length.

Cast on 70sts.

Row 1 and all alternate rows. Knit.

Row 2. K3, (pleat lace into next st, K13) 4 times, pleat lace into next st, K10.

Row 4. K4, (pleat lace into next st, K13) 4 times, pleat lace into next st, K9.

Row 6. K5, (pleat lace into next st, K13) 4 times, pleat lace into next st, K8.

Row 8. K6, (pleat lace into next st, K13) 4 times, pleat lace into next st, K7.

Row 10. K7, (pleat lace into next st, K13) 4 times, pleat lace into next st, K6.

Row 12. K8, (pleat lace into next st, K13) 4 times, pleat lace into next st, K5.

Row 14. K9, (pleat lace into next st, K13) 4 times, pleat lace into next st, K4.

Row 16. K9, (pleat lace into next st, K13) 4 times, pleat lace into next st, K4.

Row 18. K8, (pleat lace into next st, K13) 4 times, pleat lace into next st, K5.

Row 20. K7, (pleat lace into next st, K13) 4 times, pleat lace into next st, K6.

Row 22. K6, (pleat lace into next st, K13) 4 times, pleat lace into next st, K7.

Row 24. K5, (pleat lace into next st, K13) 4 times, pleat lace into next st, K8.

Row 26. K4, (pleat lace into next st, K13) 4 times, pleat lace into next st, K9.

Row 28. K3, (pleat lace into next st, K13) 4 times, pleat lace into next st, K10.

Row 29. Knit. Cast off. Make up instructions on Page 11.

3. APRICOT & CREAM COAT-HANGER

4.9m (415 holes) of double sided eyelet lace [85 holes per metre]
8ply yarn
pr 3.75mm knitting needles
padded adult coat-hanger

Note: Overlap lace by 2 holes at each end in rows 2 and 122 to neaten.
Cut 3 pieces of lace each 127 holes in length.

Cast on 21sts.

Row 1 and alternate rows. Knit.

Row 2. K1, pleat lace in next st, K8, pleat lace in next st, K8, pleat lace in next st, K1.

Row 4. K2, pleat lace in next st, K7, pleat lace in next st, K7, pleat lace in next st, K2.

Row 6. K3, pleat lace in next st, K6, pleat lace in next st, K6, pleat lace in next st, K3.

Row 8. K4, pleat lace in next st, K5, pleat lace in next st, K5, pleat lace in next st, K4.

Row 10. K5, pleat lace in next st, K4, pleat lace in next st, K4, pleat lace in next st, K5.

Row 12. K6, pleat lace in next st, K3, pleat lace in next st, K3, pleat lace in next st, K6.

Row 14. K7, pleat lace in next st, K2, pleat lace in next st, K2, pleat lace in next st, K7.

Row 16. K6, pleat lace in next st, K3, pleat lace in next st, K3, pleat lace in next st, K6.

Row 18. K5, pleat lace in next st, K4, pleat lace in next st, K4, pleat lace in next st, K5.

Row 20. K4, pleat lace in next st, K5, pleat lace in next st, K5, pleat lace in next st, K4.

Row 22. K3, pleat lace in next st, K6, pleat lace in next st, K6, pleat lace in next st, K3.

Row 24. K2, pleat lace in next st, K7, pleat lace in next st, K7, pleat lace in next st, K2.

Repeat rows 1 - 24 four more times, then rows 1 - 3 once (123 rows in all).

Cast off.

Make up instructions on Page 11.

4. GREEN & CREAM COAT-HANGER

2.4m (200 holes) of double side eyelet lace [85 holes per metre]
8ply yarn
pr 3.75mm knitting needles
padded adult coat-hanger

Note: Lace is overlapped by 2 holes each end in rows 2 and 28 to neaten. Cut 5 pieces of lace each 33 holes in length.

Cast on 70sts.

Row 1 and alternate rows. Knit.

Row 2. (Pleat lace in next st, K13) 5 times.

Row 4. K1, (pleat lace in next st, K13) 4 times, pleat lace in next st, K12.

Row 6. K2, (pleat lace in next st, K13) 4 times, pleat lace in next st, K11.

Row 8. K3, (pleat lace in next st, K13) 4 times, pleat lace in next st, K10.

Row 10. K4, (pleat lace in next st, K13) 4 times, pleat lace in next st, K9.

Row 12. K5, (pleat lace in next st, K13) 4 times, pleat lace in next st, K8.

Row 14. K6, (pleat lace in next st, K13) 4 times, pleat lace in next st, K7.

Row 16. K7, (pleat lace in next st, K13) 4 times, pleat lace in next st, K6.

Row 18. K8, (pleat lace in next st, K13) 4 times, pleat lace in next st, K5.

Row 20. K9, (pleat lace in next st, K13) 4 times, pleat lace in next st, K4.

Row 22. K10, (pleat lace in next st, K13) 4 times, pleat lace in next st, K3.

Row 24. K11, (pleat lace in next st, K13) 4 times, pleat lace in next st, K2.

Row 26. K12, (pleat lace in next st, K13) 4 times, pleat lace in next st, K1.

Row 28. (K13, pleat lace in next st) 5 times.

Row 29. Knit. Cast off. Make up instructions on Page 11.

5. ARROW HEAD COAT-HANGER

2.4m (200 holes) of double sided eyelet lace [85 holes per metre]
8ply yarn
pr 3.75mm knitting needles
padded adult coat-hanger

Note: Overlap lace by 2 holes at each end in rows 2 and 28 to neaten.
Cut lace in 5 pieces, each 33 holes in length.

Cast on 69sts.

Row 1 and alternate rows. Knit.

Row 2. K10, pleat lace in next st, K13, pleat lace in next st, K9, pleat lace in next st, K9, pleat lace in next st, K13, pleat lace in next st, K10.

Row 4. K9, pleat lace in next st, K13, pleat lace in next st, K10, pleat lace in next st, K10, pleat lace in next st, K13, pleat lace in next st, K9.

Row 6. K8, pleat lace in next st, K13, pleat lace in next st, K11, pleat lace in next st, K11, pleat lace in next st, K13, pleat lace in next st, K8.

Row 8. K7, pleat lace in next st, K13, pleat lace in next st, K12, pleat lace in next st, K12, pleat lace in next st, K13, pleat lace in next st, K7.

Row 10. K6, pleat lace in next st, K13, pleat lace in next st, K13, pleat lace in next st, K13, pleat lace in next st, K13, pleat lace in next st, K6.

Row 12. K5, pleat lace in next st, K13, pleat lace in next st, K14, pleat lace in next st, K14, pleat lace in next st, K13, pleat lace in next st, K5.

Row 14. K4, pleat lace in next st, K13, pleat lace in next st, K15, pleat lace in next st, K15, pleat lace in next st, K13, pleat lace in next st, K4.

Row 16. K4, pleat lace in next st, K13, pleat lace in next st, K15, pleat lace in next st, K15, pleat lace in next st, K13, pleat lace in next st, K4.

Row 18. K5, pleat lace in next st, K13, pleat lace in next st, K14, pleat lace in next st, K14, pleat lace in next st, K13, pleat lace in next st, K5.

Row 20. K6, pleat lace in next st, K13, pleat lace in next st, K13, pleat lace in next st, K13, pleat lace in next st, K13, pleat lace in next st, K6.

Row 22. K7, pleat lace in next st, K13, pleat lace in next st, K12, pleat lace in next st, K12, pleat lace in next st, K13, pleat lace in next st, K7.

Row 24. K8, pleat lace in next st, K13, pleat lace in next st, K11, pleat lace in next st, K11, pleat lace in next st, K13, pleat lace in next st, K8.

Row 26. K9, pleat lace in next st, K13, pleat lace in next st, K10, pleat lace in next st, K10, pleat lace in next st, K13, pleat lace in next st, K9.

Row 28. K10, pleat lace in next st, K13, pleat lace in next st, K9, pleat lace in next st, K9, pleat lace in next st, K13, pleat lace in next st, K10.

Row 29. Knit. Cast off.

Hook Pocket

COAT-HANGER MAKE UP:
HANGER: Right side out, gather each short end of the cover. Place the cover centrally over the padded hanger and over-sew the long sides together.

HOOK: Fold 40cm of eyelet lace (along the long side, just beside the lace holes) to form two fancy edges. Sew a hem to form a pocket for the wire hook. Slip lace onto hook, avoiding the holes, and glue into position.

6. DUSTY PINK & CREAM COAT-HANGER

3.6m (306 holes) of double sided eyelet lace [85 holes per metre]
8ply yarn
pr 3.75mm knitting needles
padded adult coat-hanger

Note: Overlap cut ends of side lace by 2 holes at each end in rows 6 and 22, 38 and 70, and 86 and 102; and middle lace in rows 6 and 102.
Cut 3 pieces of lace 85 holes, 102 holes and 85 holes, and use in that order.

Cast on 21sts.

Rows 1 - 5. Knit.

Row 6. K3, pleat lace into next st, K6, pleat lace into next st, K6, pleat lace into next st, K3.

Row 7. Knit.

Rows 8 - 21. Repeat rows 6 and 7 seven more times. (8 pleat rows)

Cut the 2 outside laces **ONLY** allowing extra holes for next row of lace and neatening (i.e. 4 holes).

Row 22. K3, pleat lace into next st, K6, pleat lace into next st, K6, pleat lace into next st, K3. (9 pleat rows which appears as 10 pleats)

Row 23. Knit.

Row 24. K10, pleat lace into next st, K10.

Rows 25 - 36. Repeat rows 23 and 24 six more times.

(Continued on Page 15.)

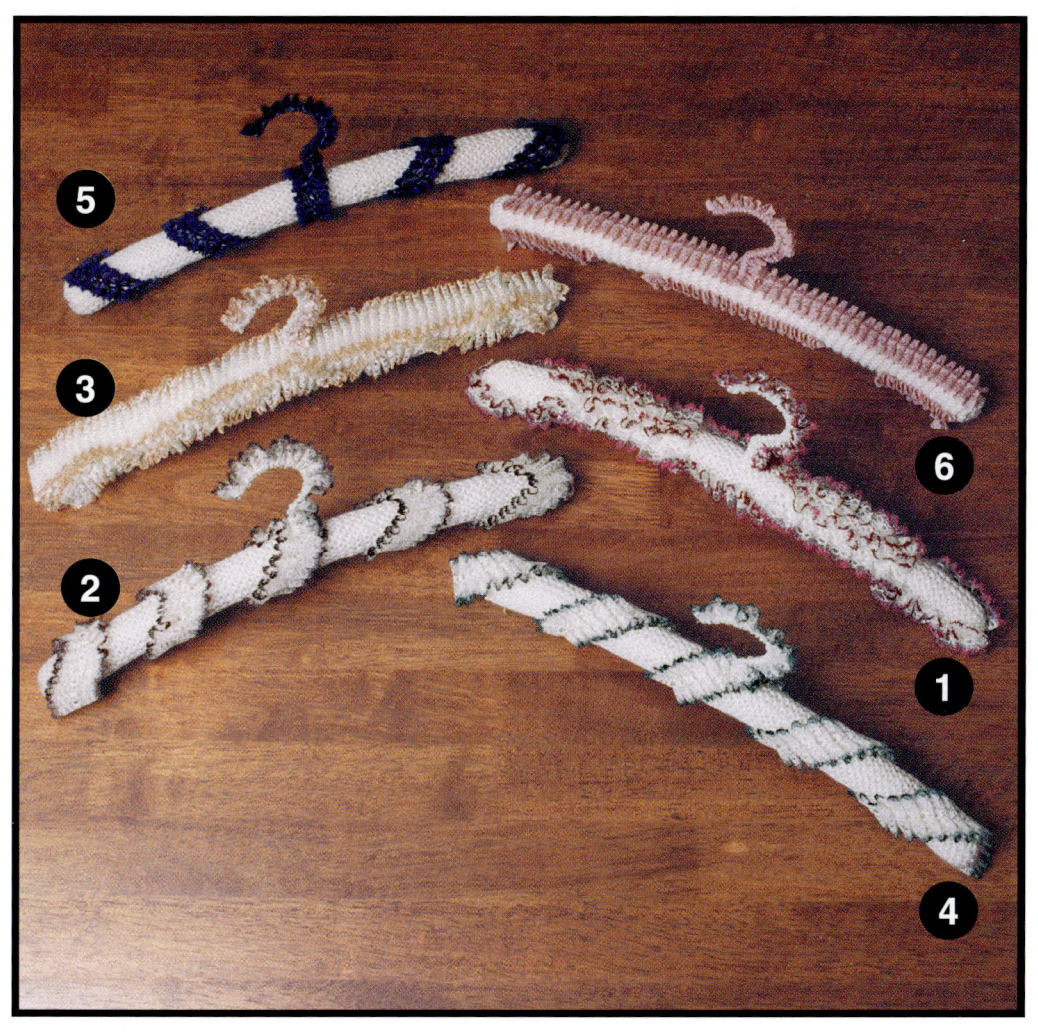

Pattern	Page
1. Maroon & Cream Coat-hanger	5
2. Brown & Cream Coat-hanger	6
3. Apricot & Cream Coat-hanger	7
4. Green & Cream Coat-hanger	9
5. Arrow Head Coat-hanger	10
6. Dusty Pink & Cream Coat-hanger	12

Pattern	Page
7. Hair Clip Tidy	15
10A. Holly Butterfly Magnet	30
10B. Lace Leaf Butterfly Magnet	31
11. Tooth Fairy	32
12. Doll's Carry Bassinet	34
13. Evening Clutch Purse	36

(Continued from Page 12.)
Row 37. Knit

Rows 38 - 69. Joining in the outside laces, repeat rows 6 and 7 sixteen more times. (16 more side pleat rows)

Cut the 2 outside laces ONLY allowing extra holes for next row of lace and neatening (i.e. 4 holes).

Row 70. K3, pleat lace into next st, K6, pleat lace into next st, K6, pleat lace into next st, K3. (Rows 38 - 70 form 17 pleat rows which appears as 18 pleats)

Rows 71 - 85. Work rows 23 - 37.

Rows 86 - 102. Joining in the outside laces, repeat rows 6 - 22 once more. (9 more side pleat rows)

Knit 3 rows. Cast off. Make up instructions on Page 11.

7. HAIR CLIP TIDY

2m (166 holes) of double sided eyelet lace [85 holes per metre]
small amounts of 8ply yarn: flesh (face)
                             2 other colours (collar / bonnet and hair)
pr 3mm knitting needles
small amount of fibre fill
1.1m of 6mm wide ribbon
scrap yarn for facial features
hair clips

HEAD Using flesh coloured yarn, cast on 15sts. (top of head)

Row 1. (K1, m1) 14 times, K1. (29sts)

Beginning with a knit row, work 18 rows in stocking stitch.

Row 20. K1, (K1, K2 tog) 9 times, K1. (20sts)

Row 21. Purl.

Row 22. (K2 tog) 10 times. (10sts)

Row 23. Purl.

Row 24. Knit.

Row 25. Purl.

Row 26. (K1, m1) 9 times, K1. (19sts)

Row 27. Purl.

Row 28. (K1, m1) 18 times, K1. (37sts)

Row 29. Purl.

Row 30. Knit. Cast off. (Shoulders made)

Right sides together, sew centre back seam. Turn right side out. Gather the cast-on stitches to form the top of the head. Stuff with fibre fill. Keeping the seam to the centre back, sew the cast-off edges together. Using 20cm of 6mm wide ribbon, thread through a few stitches at the back of the head, approximately 2cm from the top, then knot the ends to form a hanger.

COLLAR Using the same coloured yarn selected for bonnet, cast on 40sts.

Row 1. Knit in a row of lace.

Beginning with a knit row, work 6 rows of stocking stitch.

Row 8. (K2 tog) 20 times. (20sts)

Beginning with a purl row, work 3 rows of stocking stitch.

Row 12. (K2, K2 tog) 5 times. (15sts)

Row 13. Knit in a row of lace.

Row 14. Knit.

Row 15. Purl.

Break yarn and thread through the remaining stitches. Right sides together, sew centre back seam. Place the collar on the head/body, pull up yarn and secure.

BONNET Using the same colour yarn as the collar, cast on 44sts.

Row 1. (wrong side of work) Knit in a row of lace.

Row 2. Knit in a row of lace (lace will now appear on both sides).

Beginning with a knit row, work 6 rows of stocking stitch.

Row 9. (K2 tog) 22 times. (22sts)

Beginning with a purl row, knit 5 rows of stocking stitch.

Row 15. K1, (K2 tog, K2) 5 times, K1. (17sts)

Row 16. Purl.

Row 17. K1, (K2 tog, K2) 4 times. (13sts)

These 13sts are the beginning of the bonnet back flap.

Beginning with a purl row, work 16 rows of stocking stitch.

Row 34. Knit in a row of lace.

Cast off.

Right sides together, fold down bonnet back flap. Sew side edge of brim to side edge of flap. Repeat for other side. Sew 20cm of 6mm wide ribbon each side of bonnet for ties.

PLAITS Using the contrasting yarn, cut 18 pieces of yarn, each 30cm in length. Lay strands flat together, then using another piece of yarn, tie securely at one end. This becomes the top of the plait. Sew this end to the side of the head, level with the mouth. Divide the strands into 3 groups, each of 6 strands. Plait these strands and tie off securely with another piece of yarn. Trim if necessary. Repeat for other plait. Decorate with bows using 25cm of ribbon for each plait. Complete the hair by sewing and knotting a fringe across the forehead between the plaits. Using a blunt needle, unravel the strands of yarn to give a fine hair appearance.

Sew facial features of eyes, mouth and nose with scrap yarn. Place the bonnet on the head, then using a crochet hook, pull the hanger through the bonnet from the head. Sew the brim of the bonnet to the head, ensuring to cover the ends of the plaits where they join the head. Glue the fringe down if necessary. Place the hair clips on the plaits.

8. POODLE DOORSTOP

10.6m (896 holes) double sided eyelet lace [85 holes per metre]
50g each of 3 colours of 8ply yarn
1pr each 3mm and 4mm knitting needles
filled 1.25 litre soft drink bottle
50cm of 10mm wide ribbon
50cm of 3mm wide elastic
pr 12mm joggle eyes
red felt (tongue)

BODY (beginning at neck)
Using main colour yarn and 4mm needles, cast on 52sts.

Knit 2 rows.

Row 3. * K1, yarn forward, K2 tog; repeat from * to last st, K1. (17 holes for elastic)

Knit 10 rows.

Row 14. Knit in a row of lace.

Rows 15 - 17. Knit.

Repeat rows 14 to 17 thirteen more times. (14 rows of lace)

Row 70. Knit in a row of lace. (15 rows of lace)

Knit 2 rows.

Row 73. K15, K2 tog, K16, K2 tog, K15, K2 tog. (49sts)

Row 74. * K2 tog, K5; repeat from * to end. (42sts)

Knit 3 rows.

Row 78. * K2 tog, K4; repeat from * to end. (35sts)

Knit 3 rows.

Row 82. * K2 tog, K3; repeat from * to end. (28sts)

Knit 3 rows.

Row 86. * K2 tog, K2; repeat from * to end. (21sts)

Knit 3 rows.

Row 90. * K2 tog; repeat from * to last st, K1. (11sts)

Break off yarn, thread through the remaining stitches, **pull up and fasten off.**

HEAD Using main coloured yarn and 4mm needles, cast on 52sts.

Knit 3 rows.

Row 4. Knit in a row of lace.

Knit 2 rows.

Row 7. * K1, yarn forward, K2 tog; repeat from * to last st, K1. (17 ribbon holes)

Change to 3mm needles and continue as follows:

Row 8. Knit.

Row 9. K15, K2 tog, K16, K2 tog, K15, K2 tog. (49sts)

Row 10. Knit.

Row 11. * K2 tog, K5; repeat from * to end. (42sts)

Knit 3 rows.

Row 15. * K2 tog, K4; repeat from * to end. (35sts)

Knit 23 rows.

Row 39. * K2 tog, K3; repeat from * to end. (28sts)

Knit 1 row.

Row 41. * K2 tog, K2; repeat from * to end. (21sts)

Knit 1 row.

Row 43. * K2 tog; repeat from * to last st, K1. (11sts)

Row 44. Knit.

Break off yarn, thread through the remaining stitches, pull up and fasten off.

NOSE Using 3mm needles and main colour, cast on 13sts.

Knit 16 rows.

Row 17. K1, * K2 tog, K1; repeat from * to end. (9sts)

Row 18. K1, * K2 tog; repeat from * to end. (5sts - tip of nose)

Break off yarn, thread through the remaining stitches, pull up and fasten off.

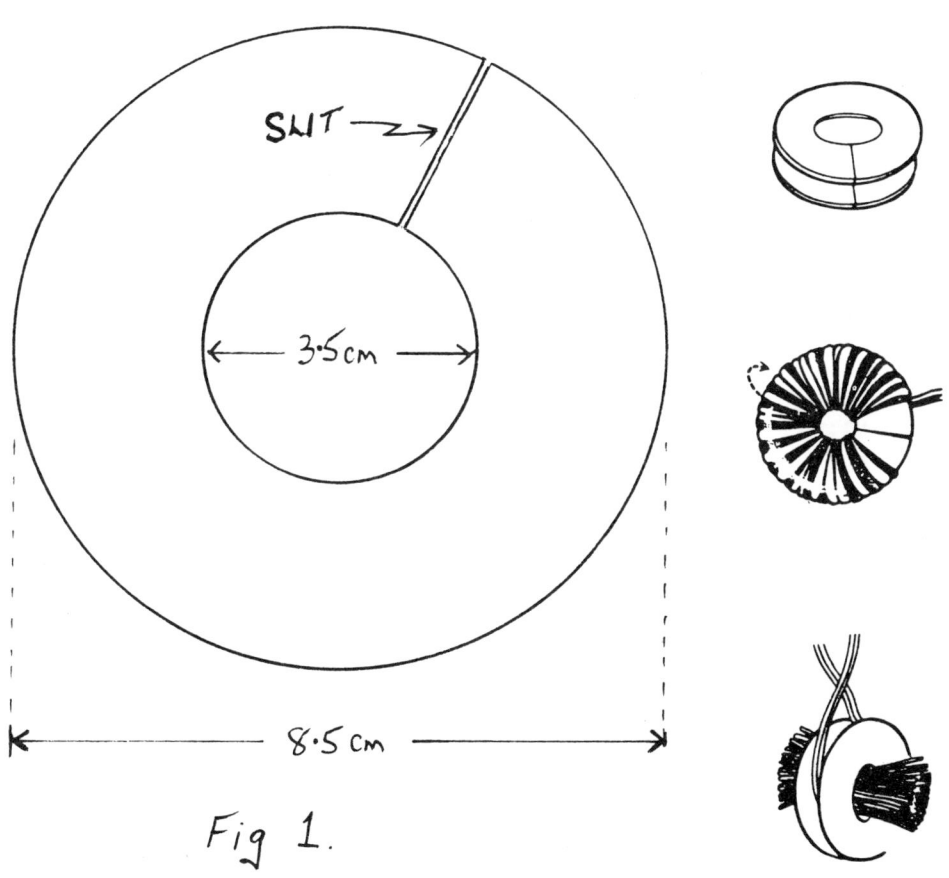

Fig 1.

POM-POMS (Make 8) *See Fig 1 on Page 21.*
Using the two contrast coloured yarns make 8 pom-poms each with a diameter of 8.5cms.
To make a pom-pom, cut two circles of cardboard 8.5cm in diameter, then cut a 3.5cm hole in the centre of each. Holding these two rings together, cut a slit through one side to the centre. Keeping the rings together, with the slits aligned, wind the yarn over the rings (drawing through slits) until the centre hole is filled. Cut the yarn between the two rings of cardboard, sliding the scissors between the two rings. Using double yarn, tie around (between the rings) and secure. Remove the rings. Trim the pom-pom, leaving the tying yarn to sew the pom-poms to body and head.

Make up:
Body
Leaving the cast-on edge open, right sides together join centre back body seam. Turn right side out. Thread elastic through the holes of the body and tie off so as to fit the neck of the bottle.
Sew a pom-pom to the centre back seam on the 3rd row of lace from the base. This is the tail. Sew on 4 more pom-poms for the legs, in pairs, on 3rd and 11th row of lace from the cast-on edge. (See colour picture opposite.) Place body on filled bottle, adjusting the elastic if necessary.

Head
Leaving the cast-on edges open, right sides together, join centre back head seam. Turn right side out. Leaving the cast-on edge open, right sides together, join the side nose seam. Turn right side out. Stuff with scrap yarn and sew to centre of face. Sew or glue on the eyes and sew a small piece of red felt in place for a mouth. Sew a pom-pom to the top of the head, and one to each side of the head to form ears. Thread the ribbon through the ribbon holes, tie into a bow at the centre front. Place the head on the bottle, overlapping the neck to conceal the elastic.

Pattern	Page
8. Poodle Doorstop	18

Pattern	Page
9. Doorstop Dolly	25

9. DOORSTOP DOLLY

** 34.3m (2914 holes) double sided eyelet lace [85 holes per metre]
110g 8ply knitting yarn
pr 4mm knitting needles
4.5mm 80cm long circular knitting needles
35cm doll with removable legs
80cm of 6mm wide ribbon
1m of 15mm wide ribbon
piece of fabric 25cm x 70cm (bottle cover)
piece of wadding 26cm x 37cm
a filled 2 litre fruit juice bottle with a handle (28cm high x 37cm around) with a secure lid
glue gun or strong glue

** If using 5 colours of lace as per the colour picture, (i.e. 3 rows each of 5 colours, with the hat and the neck using the first colour) the following amounts are required:
>   colour 1.   11.9m (1010 holes)
>   colour 2.   10m   (844 holes)
>   colour 3.   7m   (588 holes)
>   colour 4.   3.8m   (316 holes)
>   colour 5.   1.9m   (156 holes)

Notes: 4.5mm circular knitting needles are used like normal knitting needles, i.e. knitting in rows, and are used to obtain the length required to hold the large number of stitches. The pattern is NOT knitted in rounds. The larger size needles give a looser tension and a softer garment.

Tension: 20 stitches and 33 rows to 10cm over garter stitch, using 8ply yarn and 4.5mm needles.

THE BOTTLE

Remove the legs from the doll. Cut the crutch seam (between the leg openings) of the body. Using a glue gun and pushing the bottle firmly into the body of the doll, glue the doll over the filled bottle (front of bottle facing).

Glue the wadding all around the sides of the bottle, gluing and pleating the wadding around the neck of the bottle where necessary.

To make the bottle cover, fold the fabric right sides together, in half, lengthways (35cm x 25cm), then sew the side seams leaving the top open. Fold the top over 1.5cm, then another 1.5cm, and sew this hem. Turn right side out. Using a doubled gathering thread, hand sew a row of gathering stitches around this hem. Place the wadded bottle inside the bag, pull up the gathers around the neck, then secure the thread.

DRESS
Using the 4.5mm circular needles, cast on 288sts.

Row 1. Knit.

Row 2. Knit in a row of lace.

Rows 3 - 7. Knit.

Repeat rows 2 - 7 three more times. (4 rows of lace)

Row 26. Knit in a row of lace. (5 rows of lace)

Rows 27 - 30. Knit.

Row 31. K3, * K2 tog, K7; repeat from * to last 6sts, K2 tog, K4. (256sts)

Row 32. Knit in a row of lace. (6 rows of lace)

Rows 33 - 36. Knit.

Row 37. K3, * K2 tog, K6; repeat from * to last 5sts, K2 tog, K3. (224sts)

Row 38. Knit in a row of lace. (7 rows of lace)

Rows 39 - 42. Knit.

Row 43. K2, * K2 tog, K5; repeat from * to last 5sts, K2 tog, K3. (192sts)

Row 44. Knit in a row of lace. (8 rows of lace)

Rows 45 - 48. Knit.

Row 49. K2, * K2 tog, K4; repeat from * to last 4sts, K2 tog, K2. (160sts)

Row 50. Knit in a row of lace. (9 rows of lace)

Rows 51 - 54. Knit.

Row 55. K2, * K2 tog, K3; repeat from * to last 3sts, K2 tog, K1. (128sts)

Row 56. Knit in a row of lace. (10 rows of lace)

Rows 57 - 60. Knit.

Row 61. K1, * K2 tog, K2; repeat from * to last 3sts, K2 tog, K1. (96sts)

Row 62. Knit in a row of lace. (11 rows of lace)

Rows 63 - 66. Knit.

Row 67. K2, * K2 tog, K4; repeat from * to last 4sts, K2 tog, K2. (80sts)

Row 68. Knit in a row of lace. (12 rows of lace)

Rows 69 - 72. Knit.

Row 73. K2, * K2 tog, K3; repeat from * to last 3sts, K2 tog, K1. (64sts)

Row 74. Knit in a row of lace. (13 rows of lace)

Rows 75 - 78. Knit.

Row 79. K1, * K2 tog, K2; repeat from * to last 3sts, K2 tog, K1. (48sts)

Row 80. Knit in a row of lace. (14 rows of lace)

Rows 81 - 84. Knit.

Row 85. K1, * K2 tog, K1; repeat from * to last 2sts, K2 tog. (32sts)

Row 86. Knit in a row of lace. (15 rows of lace)

BODICE

Change to 4mm needles and beginning with a knit row, knit 12 rows in stocking stitch.

Row 13. (Armholes) K7, cast off next 4sts, K9, cast off next 4sts, K6. (24sts, 7sts in each back half and 10sts in front)

Row 14. P7, turn work, cast on 5sts, turn work, P10, turn work, cast on 5sts, turn work, P7. (34sts)

Row 15. Knit.

Row 16. Purl.

Row 17. Knit.

Row 18. Knit in a row of lace.

Row 19. K6, K2 tog, K3, K2 tog, K8, K2 tog, K3, K2 tog, K6. (30sts)

Row 20. Purl.

Row 21. K5, K2 tog, K2, K2 tog, K8, K2 tog, K2, K2 tog, K5. (26sts)

Row 22. Purl. Cast off.

Right sides together, sew centre back seam to waist. Turn right side out and place on doll. Sew the remainder of the back seam. Place the 15mm wide ribbon around the doll's waist, and tie in a bow at the back.

HAT

Using 4mm needles, cast on 44sts.

Row 1. Using colour 1 lace and turning the lace under by 2 holes to neaten at beginning and end of row, knit in a row of lace.

Row 2. Knit.

Row 3. Purl.

Row 4. As before in row 1, knit in a row of lace. (lace now appears on both sides)

Beginning with a purl row, work 9 rows of stocking stitch.

Row 14. Cast on 10sts, knit to end of row. (54sts)

Row 15. Cast on 10sts, purl to end of row. (64sts)

Row 16. K3, * K2 tog, K6; repeat from * to last 5sts, K2 tog, K3. (56sts)

Row 17. Purl.

Row 18. K3, * K2 tog, K5; repeat from * to last 4sts, K2 tog, K2. (48sts)

Row 19. Purl.

Row 20. K2, * K2 tog, K4; repeat from * to last 4sts, K2 tog, K2. (40sts)

Row 21. Purl.

Row 22. K2, * K2 tog, K3; repeat from * to last 3sts, K2 tog, K1. (32sts)

Row 23. Purl.

Row 24. K1, * K2 tog, K2; repeat from * to last 3sts, K2 tog, K1. (24sts)

Row 25. Purl.

Row 26. K1, * K2 tog, K1; repeat from * to last 2sts, K2 tog. (16sts)

Row 27. Purl.

Row 28. K2 tog to end. (8sts)

Cut yarn and draw through the remaining 8 stitches. Pull up and secure. Right sides together, sew centre back seam, then sew each of the side brim seams to 7 of the 10 cast-on stitches from rows 14 and 15, omitting the 3 cast-on stitches either side of the centre back seam. Turn right side out. Thread the 6mm wide ribbon through the remaining 6 cast-on stitches. Place the hat on the doll and tie the ribbon in a bow under her chin.

10. BUTTERFLY MAGNETS

10A. HOLLY BUTTERFLY

---

30 holes of double sided eyelet lace
6mm chenille stem
2 large holly leaves
2 small holly leaves
2 large stamens
magnet
strong glue

Cut a 10cm length of chenille stem. Pleat the lace onto the centre of the chenille stem, pushing the pleats close together to a length of 4cm. Fold back the chenille stem ends behind the lace and twist them together. In pairs, twist the holly wire stems into a cross shape. Glue together to form butterfly wings, having the smaller leaves to the bottom. Cut away any excess wire. Glue the stamens in place for antennae. Glue the pleated lace into position on top of the wings to form the body. Glue a magnet to centre back.

10B. LACE LEAF BUTTERFLY

42 holes of double sided eyelet lace
6mm glitter chenille stem
2 large lace leaves
2 small lace leaves
magnet
strong glue
silver glitter glue pen

Cut a 18cm length of chenille stem. Beginning mid-way along the stem, (see Fig 2) pleat the lace onto the centre of the chenille stem, pushing the pleats close together to a length of 4cm. Fold under the long end of the chenille stem. Twist the stem ends together, leaving 4cm ends to form the antennae. Bend the antennae into shape and trim if necessary. In pairs, glue the lace leaves into a cross shape to form butterfly wings, having the smaller leaves to the bottom. Cut away any excess stems. Glue the pleated lace into position on top of the wings to form the body. Glue a magnet to centre back. Highlight the wings with a glitter glue pen.

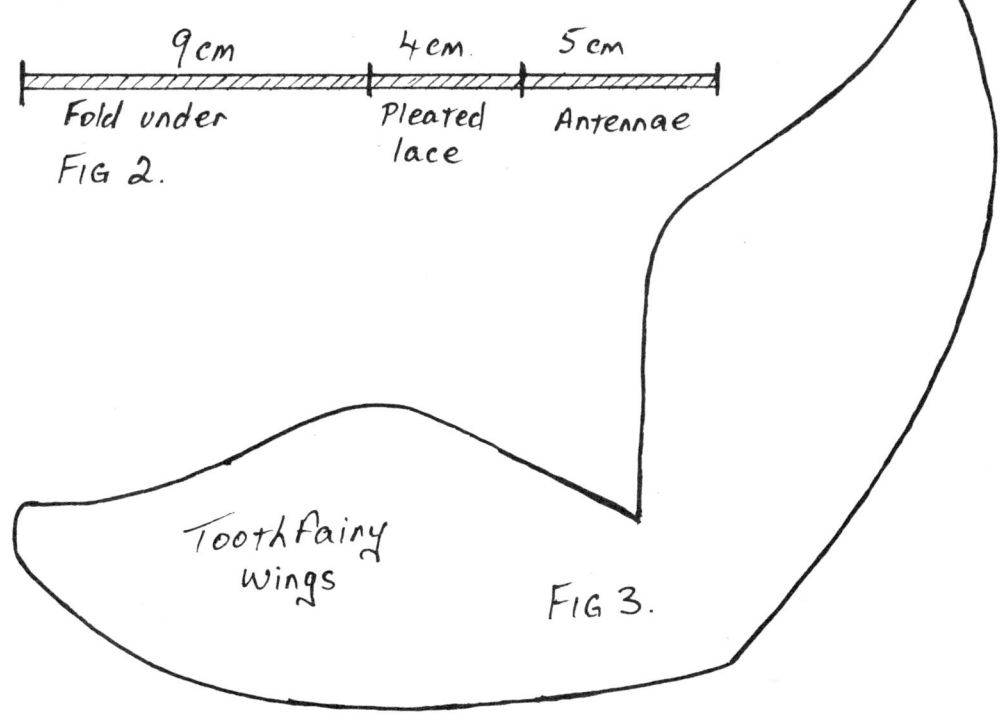

11. TOOTH FAIRY

6m (505 holes) double sided eyelet lace [85 holes per metre]
20g 8ply yarn
pr 3.75mm knitting needles
40cm of 6mm wide ribbon
25cm doll
milk bottle plastic
PVA glue
glitter

DRESS
Cast on 55sts.

Rows 1 and 2. Knit.

Row 3. Knit in a row of lace.

Rows 4 - 6. Knit.

Row 7. Knit in a row of lace.

Repeat rows 4 - 7 twice more times. (4 rows of lace)

Rows 16 and 17. Knit.

Row 18. * K9, K2 tog; repeat from * to end. (50sts)

Row 19. Knit in a row of lace. (5 rows of lace)

Rows 20 and 21. Knit.

Row 22. * K8, K2 tog; repeat from * to end. (45sts)

Row 23. Knit in a row of lace. (6 rows of lace)

Rows 24 and 25. Knit.

Row 26. * K7, K2 tog; repeat from * to end. (40sts)

Row 27. Knit in a row of lace. (7 rows of lace)

Rows 28 and 29. Knit.

Row 30. * K6, K2 tog; repeat from * to end. (35sts)

Row 31. Knit in a row of lace. (8 rows of lace)

Rows 32 and 33. Knit.

Row 34. * K5, K2 tog; repeat from * to end. (30sts)

Row 35. Knit in a row of lace. (9 rows of lace)

Rows 36 and 37. Knit.

Row 38. * K4, K2 tog; repeat from * to end. (25sts)

Row 39. Knit in a row of lace. (10 rows of lace)

Rows 40 - 48. Beginning with a knit row, work 9 rows of stocking stitch.

Row 49. P6, cast off next 2sts, P8, cast off next 2sts, P5. (21sts)

Row 50. (armholes) K6, turn work, cast on 3sts, turn work, K9, turn work, cast on 3sts, turn work, K6. (27sts)

Row 51. Purl.

Row 52. Knit.

Row 53. Knit in a row of lace.

Cast off.

Right sides together, sew centre back seam. Turn right side out.

PURSE
Cast on 9sts, and beginning with a knit row, work 18 rows of stocking stitch.

Cast off.

Right sides together, sew side seams leaving the cast-on and cast-off edges open. Turn right side out. Using 15cm of ribbon, sew an end to each side seam at the top of the purse. Beginning at centre front, thread 25cm of ribbon through the cast-on and cast-off stitches. Pull up ends and tie them in a bow.

WINGS
Using Fig 3 on Page 31, trace and cut the wings from milk bottle plastic. Paint one side of wing with PVA glue and sprinkle with glitter. When dry, complete for other side. Spray the wings with hair spray or lacquer to prevent the glitter from flaking. Sew wings to centre back seam of dress.

Place the dress on the doll (you may have to remove her arms for this procedure). Using a strand of yarn, sew a hanger to the top of inside centre back seam. When the hanger is not in use, simply tuck it inside the dress. Hang the purse off one arm.

12. DOLL'S CARRY BASSINET

4m (340 holes) double sided eyelet lace [85 holes per metre]
4m (340 holes) contrast colour double sided eyelet lace [85 holes per metre]
15g 8ply yarn
pr 3.75mm needles
1.5m of 6mm wide ribbon
plastic cordial bottle (oblong base 9cm x 12cm)
hole punch

Cut the bottle 6.5cm from the base. Discard the top part of the bottle. Remove any label from the base part and clean the plastic. Punch holes around the top of the base 5mm down from the top with the centres 7 - 8mm apart (approx. 48 holes). Because the knitting is sewn on afterwards, a few holes more or less will not matter. Using a tapestry needle or similar, work a row of blanket stitch in the holes, working 2 stitches in each hole as shown.

BLANKET STITCH

Cast on 82sts.

Row 1. Knit in a row of main colour lace.

Rows 2 and 3. Knit.

Row 4. Knit in a row of contrast colour lace. (Lace will now appear on the opposite side of work, this is the inside)

Rows 5 and 6. Knit.

Repeat rows 1 - 6 three more times. (4 rows of lace on both sides of work)

Row 25. K1, * yarn around needle, K2 tog, K1; repeat from * to end. (32 ribbon holes)

Row 26. Knit. Cast off.

Neatly over-sew the side seams together. Sew cast-on edge to the blanket stitch row. Using 75cm of ribbon, and beginning at the one side, thread the ribbon through the ribbonholes. The point of entry and exit will be the same hole. Tie ends of ribbon together in a knot. Repeat for other side, with the ribbon following the same path as the first ribbon, except the point of entry and exit will be opposite. Pull up draw strings and tie in a knot.

13 EVENING CLUTCH PURSE

7.8m (660 holes) double sided eyelet lace [85 holes per metre]
8ply yarn
pr 3mm knitting needles
clutch purse frame (15 x 5cm)
fabric lining to match yarn (approx. 17 x 24cm)
strong sewing thread

Cast on 26sts.

Rows 1 - 3. Knit.

Row 4. Knit in a row of lace.

Repeat the last 4 rows twice more, placing a marker at the beginning and end of the third lace row.

Repeat rows 1 - 4 sixteen more times, placing a marker at the beginning and end of the nineteenth lace row.

Repeat rows 1 - 4 three more times. (22 rows of lace)

Knit 2 rows and cast off loosely. Weave in all loose ends.

Cut a piece of liner fabric 2cm longer than the knitting and 2cm wider than the frame. Right sides together, fold liner in half lengthways. Sew a 1cm seam at each side leaving the last 6cm open to sew into frame. Iron a 1cm hem around the remaining edges and sew.

Right sides together, fold knitting in half lengthways and beginning at fold, sew side seams to markers, leaving the cast-on edge and cast-off edges open to sew to frame.

Wrong sides together place liner inside knitting and hand sew the unsewn edges together, forming a lined pocket. Sew pocket to frame with a strong thread.